COVID-19 HELPERS

by Beth Bacon and Kary Lee

BLAIR

905 W. Main Street, Suite 19 D-1
Durham, NC 27701

Text © 2020 by Beth Bacon
Pictures © 2020 by Kary Lee

Library of Congress Control Number: 2020945378
ISBN: 978-1-949467-61-1 (paperback)
ISBN: 978-1-949467-60-4 (hardcover)

In the spring of 2020, something very unusual happened.

Children around the world
stopped going to school.

They stopped playing
in the parks. They stopped
going to sports games,

**and movie theaters,
and birthday parties.**

In the spring of 2020, it seemed like kids everywhere were doing nothing.

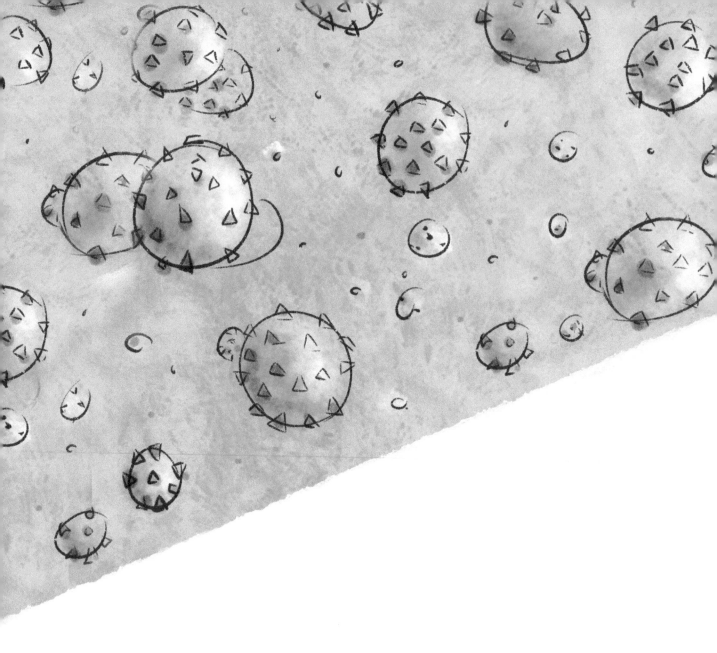

They were doing something very
important. They were helping to
fight a brand-new disease.

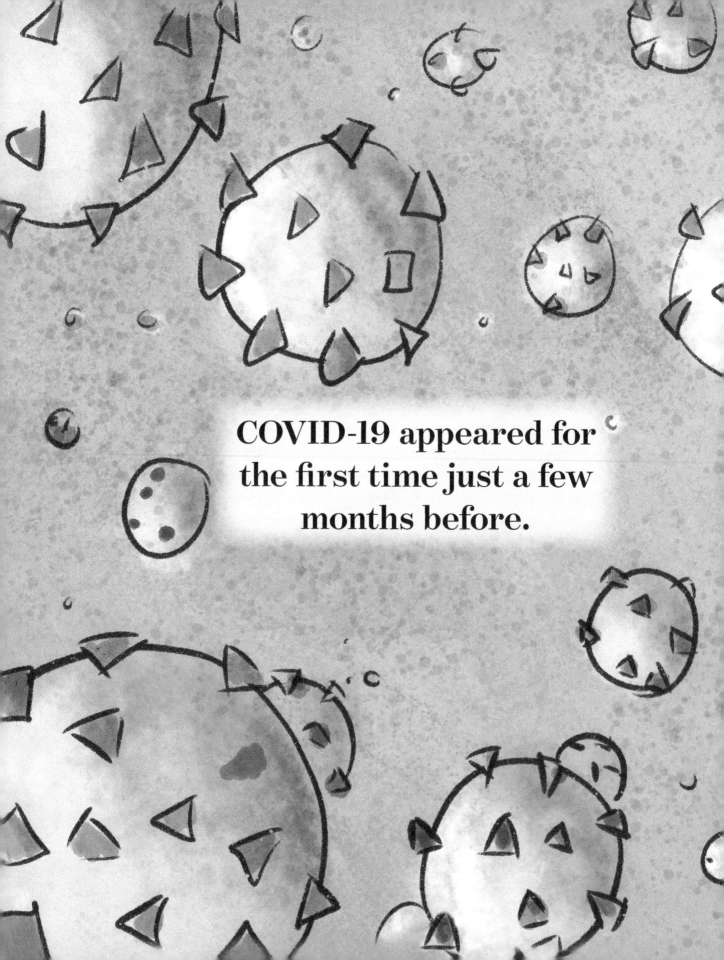

COVID-19 appeared for the first time just a few months before.

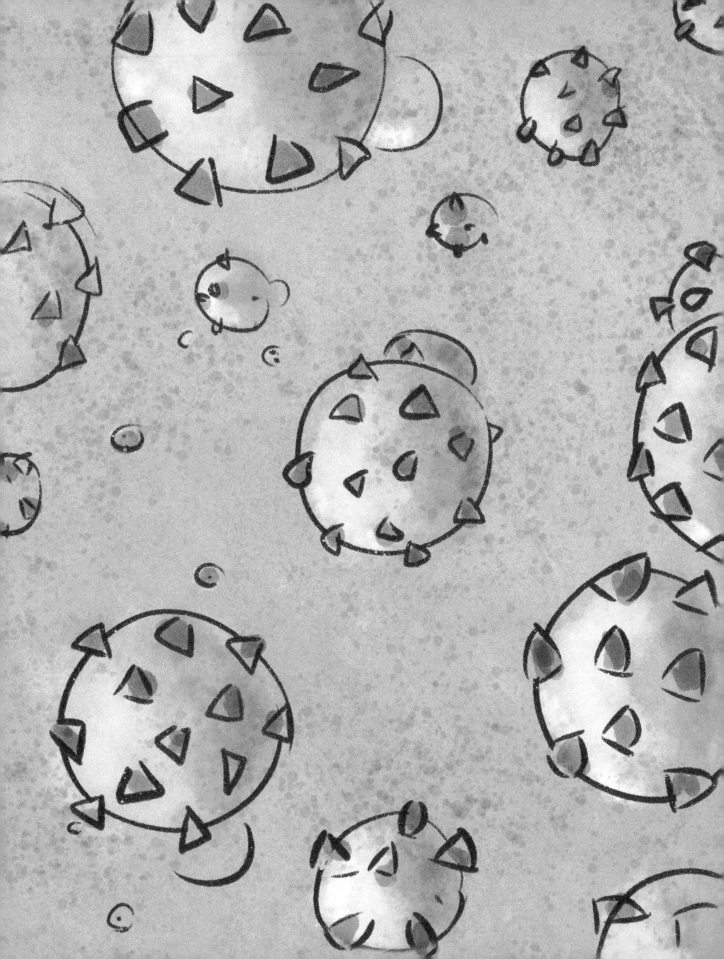

Most people were
not harmed by
the virus.

But it made some
people very sick.

Because it was new, doctors
did not have a cure.

So people everywhere began to help.

Healthcare workers helped sick people recover.

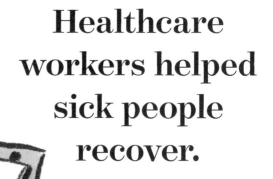

Researchers helped to discover new medicines.

Leaders helped
by making
new plans.

Reporters
helped share
the news.

Farmers and grocers helped

by making sure there was healthy food to eat.

Truck drivers helped by transporting supplies.

Garbage collectors helped by keeping communities clean.

When they went to the market, shoppers helped by wearing masks and staying six feet apart.

And kids helped, too,
just by staying at home.

It may seem like
staying at home was doing
nothing. But this was an
important job.

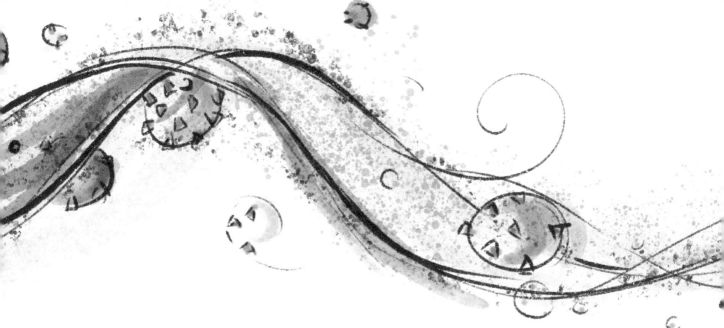

COVID-19 is spread by tiny droplets in the air.

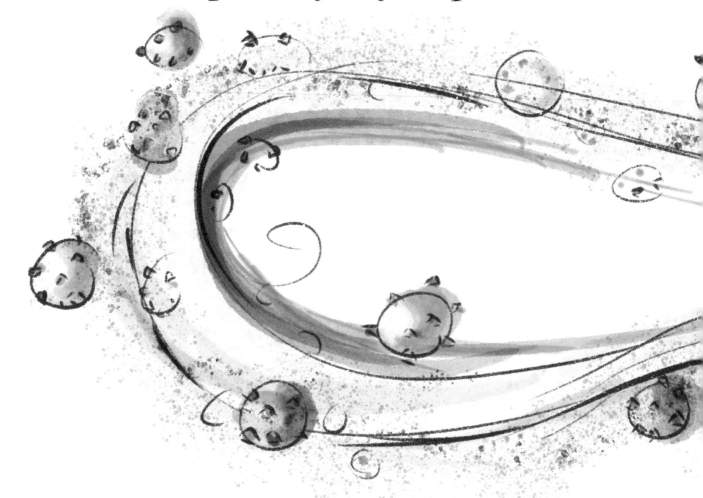

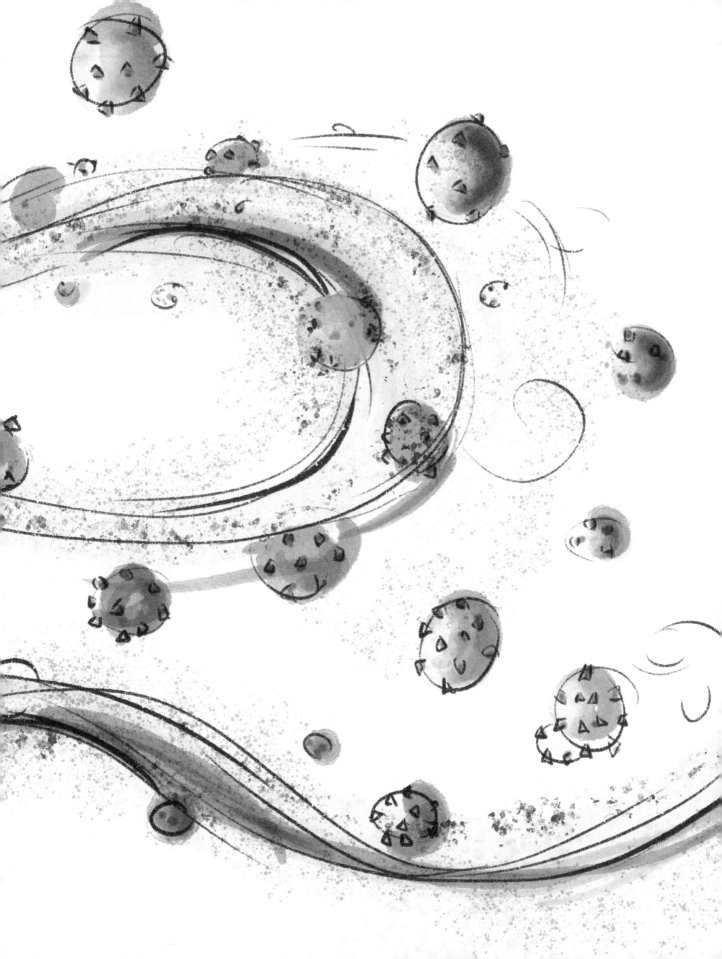

When more people get together, more droplets fill the air.

When fewer people get together, fewer droplets fill the air.

With fewer droplets in the air, fewer people may get sick.

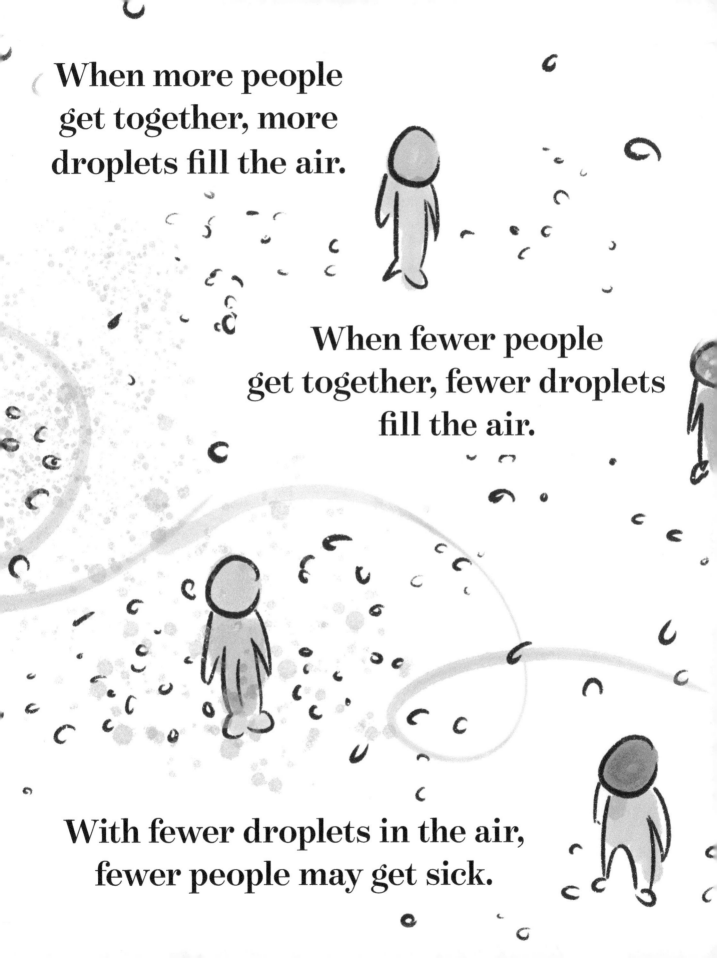

Soon, researchers will find a cure.

Until they do,
everyone is helping.

Everyone, including
kids like you.

ABOUT THE SPONSOR

Emory Global Health Institute (EGHI)
brings together diverse disciplines to tackle
global health issues.

In 2020, COVID-19 began spreading around the
United States. Inspired by his grandchildren's
questions about the pandemic, Dr. Jeffrey Koplan,
the director of EGHI and vice president for global
health at Emory University, believed children's
books could provide some answers. So he and his
colleagues decided to hold a competition. Writers
and illustrators submitted 260 stories to EGHI, and
this book, *COVID-19 Helpers*, won first place.

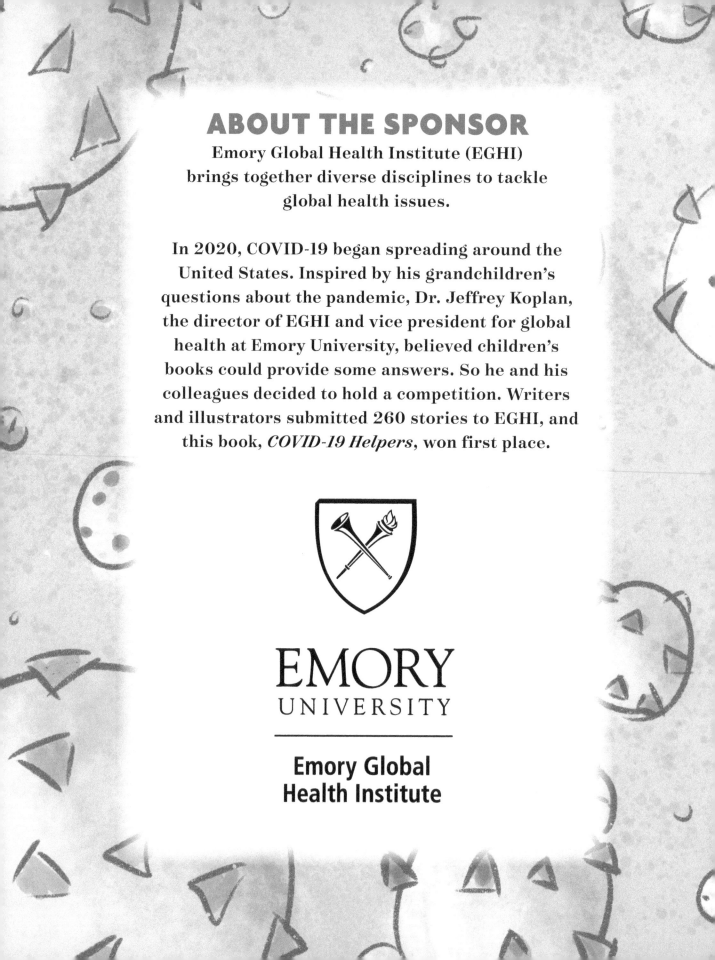

EMORY
UNIVERSITY

**Emory Global
Health Institute**

ABOUT THE AUTHOR

When Beth Bacon was young, she loved to read. Now she loves to write. Her other books include *I Hate Reading*, *The Worst Book Ever*, *The Book No One Wants To Read*, and *Blank Space*.

Beth earned an MFA in writing for children from Vermont College of Fine Arts. She also has a degree in communications from NYU and a degree in literature from Harvard. She and her husband have two sons, a cat, and, lately, lots of foreign exchange students.

BethBaconAuthor.com

ABOUT THE ILLUSTRATOR

As a kid, if Kary Lee wasn't in her backyard painting or tapping at the typewriter, she was most likely directing (bossing around) the neighborhood kids in one of her screenplays.

After college, she landed a job as an art director because she liked the bossy part. She took a painting class and won a book illustration award. Five books and a Mom's Choice Award later, she's never looked back. Kary lives in Seattle with her husband, Charles, and a backyard bunny.

KaryLeeStudios.com

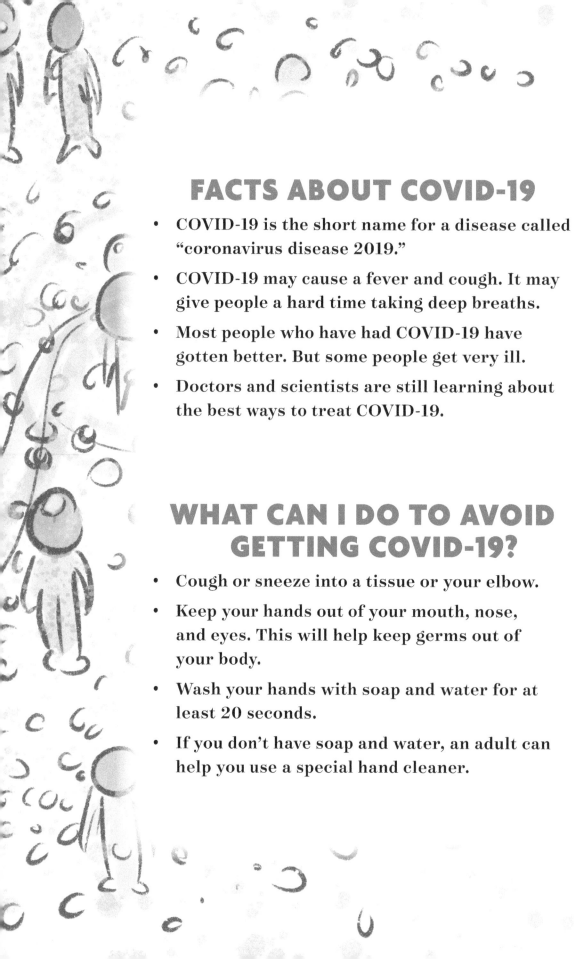

FACTS ABOUT COVID-19

- COVID-19 is the short name for a disease called "coronavirus disease 2019."

- COVID-19 may cause a fever and cough. It may give people a hard time taking deep breaths.

- Most people who have had COVID-19 have gotten better. But some people get very ill.

- Doctors and scientists are still learning about the best ways to treat COVID-19.

WHAT CAN I DO TO AVOID GETTING COVID-19?

- Cough or sneeze into a tissue or your elbow.

- Keep your hands out of your mouth, nose, and eyes. This will help keep germs out of your body.

- Wash your hands with soap and water for at least 20 seconds.

- If you don't have soap and water, an adult can help you use a special hand cleaner.